CARYL CHURCHILL

Caryl Churchill has written for the stage, television and radio. Her stage plays include *Owners* (Royal Court Theatre Upstairs, 1972); *Objections to Sex and Violence* (Royal Court, 1975); *Light Shining in Buckinghamshire* (Joint Stock on tour incl. Theatre Upstairs, 1976); *Vinegar Tom* (Monstrous Regiment on tour, incl. Half Moon and ICA, 1976); *Traps* (Theatre Upstairs, 1977), *Cloud Nine* (Joint Stock on tour incl. Royal Court, London, 1979, then Theatre de Lys, New York, 1981); *Three More Sleepless Nights* (Soho Poly and Theatre Upstairs, 1980); *Top Girls* (Royal Court, London, then Public Theatre, New York, 1982); *Fen* (Joint Stock on tour, incl. Almeida and Royal Court, London, then Public Theatre, New York, 1983); *Softcops* (RSC at the Pit, 1984); *A Mouthful of Birds* with David Lan (Joint Stock on tour, incl. Royal Court, 1986); *Serious Money* (Royal Court and Wyndham's, London, then Public Theatre, New York, 1987); *Icecream* (Royal Court, 1989); *Mad Forest* (Central School of Speech and Drama, then Royal Court, 1990); *Lives of the Great Poisoners* with Orlando Gough and Ian Spink (Second Stride on tour, incl. Riverside Studios, London, 1991); *The Skriker* (Royal National Theatre, 1994); *Thyestes* translated from Seneca (Royal Court Theatre Upstairs, 1994); *Hotel* with Orlando Gough and Ian Spink (Second Stride on tour, incl. The Place, London, 1997); *This is a Chair* (London International Festival of Theatre at the Royal Court, 1997); *Blue Heart* (Joint Stock on tour, incl. Royal Court Theatre, 1997); *Far Away* (Royal Court Theatre Upstairs, 2000, and Albery, London, 2001, then New York Theatre Workshop, 2002); *A Number* (Royal Court Theatre Downstairs, 2002, then New York Theatre Workshop, 2004).

CARYL CHURCHILL

A Number

THEATRE
COMMUNICATIONS GROUP
New York

A Number first published by Theatre Communications Group, Inc., 520 Eighth Avenue, 24th Floor, New York, NY 10018-4156, by special arrangement with Nick Hern Books Limited.

A Number first published in 2002 as a paperback original by Nick Hern Books, 14 Larden Road, London W3 7ST in association with the Royal Court Theatre

A Number copyright©2002 by Caryl Churchill Ltd

Caryl Churchill has asserted her right to be identified as the author of this work

ISBN-13: 978-1-55936-225-2
ISBN-10: 1-55936-225-1

A CIP catalogue record for this book is available from the Library of Congress

CAUTION All rights whatsoever in this play are strictly reserved. Requests to reproduce the text in whole or in part should be addressed to Nick Hern Books.

Amateur Performing Rights Applications for performance in excerpt or in full by non-professionals in English throughout the world (excluding the United States of America and Canada) should be addressed to Samuel French Ltd, 52 Fitzroy Street, London W1T 5JR, *fax* 020 7387 2161, or their overseas agents.

Professional Performing Rights Applications for performance by professionals in any medium and in any language throughout the world and for amateur and stock rights in the United States of America and Canada should be addressed to Casarotto Ramsay and Associates Ltd, National House, 60-66 Wardour Street, London W1V 4ND, *e-mail* agents@casarotto.uk.com

TCG books are exclusively distributed to the book trade by Consortium Book Sales and Distribution, 1045 Westgate Drive, St. Paul MN, 55114.

First TCG edition, April 2003.
Third Printing, September 2005.

A Number was first performed by Michael Gambon
and Daniel Craig at the Royal Court Theatre, London,
on 23 September 2002. The play was directed by
Stephen Daldry and designed by Ian MacNeil. Lighting
was designed by Rick Fisher and Ian Dickinson was the
sound designer.

US premiere by New York Theatre Workshop.

Characters

SALTER, *a man in his early sixties*

BERNARD, *his son, forty*

BERNARD, *his son, thirty-five*

MICHAEL BLACK, *his son, thirty-five*

The play is for two actors. One plays Salter, the other his sons.
The scene is the same throughout, it's where Salter lives.

1

SALTER, *a man in his early sixties and his son* BERNARD (B2), *thirty-five.*

B2	A number
SALTER	you mean
B2	a number of them, of us, a considerable
SALTER	say
B2	ten, twenty
SALTER	didn't you ask?
B2	I got the impression
SALTER	why didn't you ask?
B2	I didn't think of asking.
SALTER	I can't think why not, it seems to me it would be the first thing you'd want to know, how far has this thing gone, how many of these things are there?
B2	Good, so if it ever happens to you
SALTER	no you're right
B2	no it was stupid, it was shock, I'd known for a week before I went to the hospital but it was still

SALTER	it is, I am, the shocking thing is that there *are* these, not how many but at all
B2	even one
SALTER	exactly, even one, a twin would be a shock
B2	a twin would be a surprise but a number
SALTER	a number any number is a shock.
B2	You said things, these things
SALTER	I said?
B2	you called them things. I think we'll find they're people.
SALTER	Yes of course they are, they are of course.
B2	Because I'm one.
SALTER	No.
B2	Yes. Why not? Yes.
SALTER	Because they're copies
B2	copies? they're not
SALTER	copies of you which some mad scientist has illegally
B2	how do you know that?
SALTER	I don't but
B2	what if someone else is the one, the first one, the real one and I'm

SALTER	no because
B2	not that I'm *not* real which is why I'm saying they're not things, don't call them
SALTER	just wait, because I'm your father.
B2	You know that?
SALTER	Of course.
B2	It was all a normal, everything, birth
SALTER	you think I wouldn't know if I wasn't your father?
B2	Yes of course I was just for a moment there, but they are all still people like twins are all, quins are all
SALTER	yes I'm sorry
B2	we just happen to have identical be identical identical genetic
SALTER	sorry I said things, I didn't mean anything by that, it just
B2	no forget it, it's nothing, it's
SALTER	because of course for me you're the
B2	yes I know what you meant, I just, because of course I want them to be things, I do think they're things, I don't think they're, of course I *do* think they're them just as much as I'm me but I. I don't know what I think, I feel terrible.
SALTER	I wonder if we can sue.

B2	Sue? who?
SALTER	Them, whoever did it. Who did you see?
B2	Just some young, I don't know, younger than me.
SALTER	So who did it?
B2	He's dead, he was some old and they've just found the records and they've traced
SALTER	so we sue the hospital.
B2	Maybe. Maybe we can.
SALTER	Because they've taken your cells
B2	but when how did they?
SALTER	when you were born maybe or later you broke your leg when you were two you were in the hospital, some hairs or scrapings of your skin
B2	but they didn't damage
SALTER	but it's you, part of you, the value
B2	the value of those people
SALTER	yes
B2	and what is the value of
SALTER	there you are, who knows, priceless, and they belong
B2	no
SALTER	they belong to you, they should belong to you, they're made from your

B2	they should
SALTER	they've been stolen from you and you should get your rights
B2	but is it
SALTER	what? is it money? is it something you can put a figure on? put a figure on it.
B2	This is purely
SALTER	yes
B2	suppose each person was worth ten thousand pounds
SALTER	a hundred
B2	a hundred thousand?
SALTER	they've taken a person away from you
B2	times the number of people
SALTER	which we don't know
B2	but a number a fairly large say anyway ten
SALTER	a million is the least you should take, I think it's more like half a million each person because what they've done they've damaged your uniqueness, weakened your identity, so we're looking at five million for a start.
B2	Maybe.
SALTER	Yes, because how dare they?

B2	We'd need to be able to prove
SALTER	we prove you're genetically my son genetically and then
B2	because there's no doubt
SALTER	no doubt at all. I suppose you didn't see one?
B2	One what? of them?
SALTER	of these people
B2	no I think they'd keep us apart wouldn't they so we don't spoil like contaminate the crime scene so you don't tell each other I have nightmares oh come to think of it I have nightmares and he might have said no if he was asked in the first place
SALTER	because they need to find out
B2	yes how much we're the same, not just how tall we are or do we get asthma but what do you call your dog, why did you leave your wife you don't even know the answer to these questions.
SALTER	So you didn't suddenly suddenly see
B2	what suddenly see myself coming round the corner
SALTER	because that could be
B2	like seeing yourself on the camera in a shop or you hear yourself on the

answering machine and you think god is that what I

SALTER   but more than that, it'd be it'd be

B2   don't they say you die if you meet yourself?

SALTER   walk round the corner and see yourself you could get a heart attack. Because if that's me over there who am I?

B2   Yes but it's not me over there

SALTER   no I know

B2   it's like having a twin that's all it's just

SALTER   I know what it is.

B2   I think I'd like to meet one. It's an adventure isn't it and you're part of science. I wouldn't be frightened to meet any number.

SALTER   I don't know.

B2   They're all your sons.

SALTER   I don't want a number of sons, thank you, you're plenty, I'm fine.

B2   Maybe after they've found everything out they'll let us meet. They'll have a party for us, we can

SALTER   I'm not going to drink with those doctors. But maybe you're right you're right, take it in a positive spirit.

ONE   17

B2	There is a thing
SALTER	what's that?
B2	a thing that puzzles me a little
SALTER	what's that?
B2	I did get the impression and I know I may be wrong because maybe I was in shock but I got the impression there was this batch and we were all in it. I was in it.
SALTER	No because you're my son.
B2	No but we were all
SALTER	I explained already
B2	but I wasn't being quite open with you because I'm confused because it's a shock but I want to know what happened
SALTER	they stole
B2	no but what happened
SALTER	I don't
B2	because they said that none of us was the original.
SALTER	They said that?
B2	I think
SALTER	I think you're mistaken because you're confused
B2	you think

SALTER	you need to get back to them
B2	well I'll do that. But I think that's what they meant
SALTER	it's not what they meant
B2	ok. But that's my impression, that none of us is the original.
SALTER	Then who? do they know?
B2	they're not saying, they just say we were all
SALTER	they're not saying?
B2	so if I was your son the original would be your son too which is nonsense so
SALTER	does that follow?
B2	so please if you're not my father that's fine. If you couldn't have children or my mother, and you did in vitro or I don't know what you did I really think you should tell me.
SALTER	Yes, that's what it was.
B2	That's all right.
SALTER	Yes I know.
B2	Thank you for telling me.
SALTER	Yes.
B2	It's better to know.
SALTER	Yes.
B2	So don't be upset.

ONE   19

SALTER   No.

B2   You are though

SALTER   Well.

B2   I'm fine about it. I'm not quite sure what I'm fine about. There was some other person this original some baby or cluster or and there were a number a number of us made somehow and you were one of the people who acquired, something like that.

SALTER   It wasn't

B2   don't worry

SALTER   because the thing is you see that isn't what happened. I am your father, it was by an artificial the forefront of science but I am genetically.

B2   That's great.

SALTER   Yes.

B2   So I know the truth and you're still my father and that's fine.

SALTER   Yes.

B2   So what about this original? I don't quite I don't

SALTER   There was someone.

B2   There was what kind of someone?

SALTER   There was a son.

B2   A son of yours?

SALTER	Yes.
B2	So when was that?
SALTER	That was some time earlier.
B2	Some time before I was born there was
SALTER	another son, yes, a first
B2	who what, who died
SALTER	who died, yes
B2	and you wanted to replace him
SALTER	I wanted
B2	instead of just having another child you wanted
SALTER	because your mother was dead too
B2	but she died when I was born, I thought she
SALTER	well I'm telling you what happened.
B2	So what happened?
SALTER	So they'd been killed in a carcrash and
B2	my mother and this
SALTER	carcrash
B2	when was this? how old was the child, was he
SALTER	four, he was four
B2	and you wanted him back
SALTER	yes

B2	so I'm just him over again.
SALTER	No but you are you because that's who you are but I wanted one just the same because that seemed to me the most perfect
B2	but another child might have been better
SALTER	no I wanted the same
B2	but I'm not him
SALTER	no but you're just the way I wanted
B2	but I could have been a different person not like him I
SALTER	how could you? if I'd had a different child that wouldn't be you, would it. You're this one.
B2	I'm just a copy. I'm not the real one.
SALTER	You're the only one.
B2	What do you mean only, there's all the others, there's
SALTER	but I didn't know that, that wasn't part of the deal. They were meant to make one of you not a whole number, they stole that, we'll deal with, it's something for lawyers. But you're what I wanted, you're the one.
B2	Did you give me the same name as him?
SALTER	Does it make it worse?
B2	Probably.

2

SALTER *and his other son* BERNARD (B1), *forty.*

SALTER   So they stole – don't look at me – they stole your genetic material and

B1   no

SALTER   they're the ones you want to

B1   no

SALTER   because what ten twenty twenty copies of you walking round the streets

B1   no

SALTER   which was nothing to do with me whatsoever and I think you and I should be united on this.

B1   Let me look at you.

SALTER   You've been looking at me all the

B1   let me look at you.

SALTER   Bit older.

B1   No because your father's not young when you're small is he, he's not any age, he's more a power. He's a dark dark power which is why my heart, people pay trainers to get it up to this speed, but is it because my body recognises or because I'm told? because if I'd seen you in the street I don't think I'd've stopped and shouted Daddy. But you'd've known me wouldn't you. Unless you thought I was one of the others.

SALTER   It's a long time.

B1   Can we talk about what you did?

SALTER   Yes of course. I'm not sure where what

B1   about you sent me away and had this other one made from some bit of my body some

SALTER   it didn't hurt you

B1   what bit

SALTER   I don't know what

B1   not a limb, they clearly didn't take a limb like a starfish and grow

SALTER   a speck

B1   or half of me chopped through like a worm and grow the other

SALTER   a scraping cells a speck a speck

B1   a speck yes because we're talking that microscope world of giant blobs and globs

SALTER   that's all

B1   and they take this painless scrape this specky little cells of me and kept that and you threw the rest of me away

SALTER	no
B1	and had a new one made
SALTER	no
B1	yes
SALTER	yes
B1	yes
SALTER	yes of course, you know I did, I'm not attempting to deny, I thought it was the best thing to do, it seemed a brilliant it was the only
B1	brilliant?
SALTER	it seemed
B1	to get rid
SALTER	it wasn't perfect. It was the best I could do, I wasn't very I was I was always and it's a blur to be honest but it was I promise you the best
B1	and this copy they grew of me, that worked out all right?
SALTER	There were failures of course, inevitable
B1	dead ones
SALTER	in the test tubes the dishes, I was told they didn't all
B1	but they finally got a satisfactory a bouncing

SALTER	yes but they lied to me because they didn't tell me
B1	in a cradle
SALTER	all those others, they stole
B1	and he looked just like me did he indistinguishable from
SALTER	yes
B1	so it worked out very well. And this son lives and breathes?
SALTER	yes
B1	talks and fucks? eats and walks? swims and dreams and exists somewhere right now yes does he? exist now?
SALTER	yes
B1	still exists
SALTER	yes of course
B1	happily?
SALTER	well mostly you could say
B1	as happily as most people?
SALTER	yes I think
B1	because most people are happy I read in the paper. Did it cost a lot of money?
SALTER	the procedure? to get?
B1	the baby

SALTER	yes.
B1	Were we rich?
SALTER	Not rich.
B1	No, I don't remember anything rich. A lot of dust under the bed those heaps of fluff you get don't you if you look if you go under there and lie in it.
SALTER	No, we weren't. But I managed. I was spending less.
B1	You made an effort.
SALTER	I did and for that money you'd think I'd get exclusive
B1	they ripped you off
SALTER	because one one was the deal and they
B1	what do you expect?
SALTER	from you too they it's you they, just so they can do some scientific some research some do you get asthma do you have a dog what do you call it do you
B1	Who did you think it was at the door? did you think it was one of the others or your son or
SALTER	I don't know the others
B1	you know your son
SALTER	I know
B1	your son the new

SALTER	yes of course
B1	you know him
SALTER	yes I wouldn't think he was you, no.
B1	You wouldn't think it was him having a bad day.
SALTER	You look very well.
B1	But it could have been one of the others?
SALTER	Yes because that's what I was thinking about, how could the doctors, I think there's money to be made out of this.
B1	I've not been lucky with dogs. I had this black and tan bitch wouldn't do what it's told, useless. Before that I had a lurcher they need too much running about. Then a friend of mine went inside could I look after, battle from day one with that dog, rottweiler pit bull I had to throw a chair, you could hit it with a belt it kept coming back. I'd keep it shut up in the other room and it barks so you have to hit it, I was glad when it bit a girl went to pat it and straight off to the vet, get rid of this one it's a bastard. My friend wasn't pleased but he shouldn't have gone in the postoffice.
SALTER	No that's right. I've never wanted a dog.
B1	Don't patronise me
SALTER	I'm not I'm not
B1	you don't know what you're doing

SALTER   I just

B1   because you go in a pub someone throws his beer in your face you're supposed to say sorry, he only had three stitches I'm a very restrained person. Because this minute we sit here there's somebody a lot of them but think of one on the electric bedsprings or water poured down his throat and jump on his stomach. There's a lot of wicked people. So that's why. And you see them all around you. You go down the street and you see their faces and you think you don't fool me I know what you're capable of. So don't start anything.

SALTER   I think what we need is a good solicitor.

B1   What I like about a dog it stops people getting after you, they're not going to come round in the night. But they make the place stink because I might want to stay out a few days and when I get back I might want to stay in a few days and a dog can become a tyrant to you.

           Silence.

           Hello daddy daddy daddy, daddy hello.

SALTER   Nobody regrets more than me the completely unforeseen unforeseeable which isn't my fault and does make it more upsetting but what I did did seem at the time the only and also it's a tribute, I could have had a different one, a new child altogether that's what most

	people but I wanted you again because I thought you were the best.
B1	It wasn't me again.
SALTER	No but the same basic the same raw materials because they were perfect. You were the most beautiful baby everyone said. As a child too you were very pretty, very pretty child.
B1	You know when I used to be shouting.
SALTER	No.
B1	When I was there in the dark. I'd be shouting.
SALTER	No.
B1	Yes, I'd be shouting dad dad
SALTER	Was this some time you had a bad dream or?
B1	shouting on and on
SALTER	I don't think I
B1	shouting and shouting
SALTER	no
B1	and you never came, nobody ever came
SALTER	so was this after your mum
B1	after my mum was dead this was after
SALTER	because you were very little when she
B1	yes because I can only remember
SALTER	you were maybe two when she

B1   and I remember her sitting there, she was there

SALTER   you remember so early?

B1   she'd be there but she wouldn't help stop anything

SALTER   I'm surprised

B1   so when I was shouting what I want to know

SALTER   but when was this

B1   I want to know if you could hear me or not because I never knew were you hearing me and not coming or could you not hear me and if I shouted loud enough you'd come

SALTER   I can't have heard you, no

B1   or maybe there was no one there at all and you'd gone out so no matter how hard I shouted there was no one there

SALTER   no that wouldn't have

B1   so then I'd stop shouting but it was worse

SALTER   because I hardly ever

B1   and I didn't dare get out of bed to go and see

SALTER   I don't think this can have

B1   because if there was nobody there that would be terrifying and if you were there

	that might be worse but it's something I wonder
SALTER	no
B1	could you hear me shouting?
SALTER	no I don't
B1	no
SALTER	no I don't think this happened in quite the
B1	what?
SALTER	because I'd
B1	again and again and again, every night I'd be
SALTER	no
B1	so you didn't hear?
SALTER	no but you can't have
B1	yes I was shouting, are you telling me you didn't
SALTER	no of course I didn't
B1	you didn't
SALTER	no
B1	you weren't sitting there listening to me shouting
SALTER	no
B1	you weren't out

SALTER	no
B1	so I needed to shout louder.
SALTER	Of course sometimes everyone who's had children will tell you sometimes you put them to bed and they want another story and you say goodnight now and go away and they call out once or twice and you say no go to sleep now and they might call out again and they go to sleep.
B1	The other one. Your son. My brother is he? my little twin.
SALTER	Yes.
B1	Has he got a child?
SALTER	No.
B1	Because if he had I'd kill it.
SALTER	No, he hasn't got one.
B1	So when you opened the door you didn't recognise me.
SALTER	No because
B1	Do you recognise me now?
SALTER	I know it's you.
B1	No but look at me.
SALTER	I have. I am.
B1	No, look in my eyes. No, keep looking. Look.

3

SALTER *and* BERNARD (B2).

B2	Not like me at all
SALTER	not like
B2	well like like but not identical not
SALTER	not identical no not
B2	because what struck me was how different
SALTER	yes I was struck
B2	you couldn't mistake
SALTER	no no not at all I knew at once it wasn't
B2	though of course he is older if I was older
SALTER	but even then you wouldn't
B2	I wouldn't be identical
SALTER	no no not at all no, you're a different
B2	just a bit like
SALTER	well bound to be a bit
B2	because for a start I'm not frightening.
SALTER	So what did he want did he

B2	no nothing really, not frightening not
SALTER	he didn't hit you?
B2	hit? god no, hit me? do you think?
SALTER	well he
B2	he could have done yes, no he shouted
SALTER	shouted
B1	shouted and rambled really, rambled he's not entirely
SALTER	no, well
B2	so that's what, his childhood, his life, his childhood
SALTER	all kinds of
B2	has made him a nutter really is what I think I mean not a nutter but he's
SALTER	yes yes I'm not, yes he probably is.
B2	He says all kinds of wild
SALTER	yes
B2	so you don't know what to believe.
SALTER	And how did it end up, are you on friendly
B2	friendly no
SALTER	not
B2	no no we ended up

38 A NUMBER

SALTER   yes

B2   we ended as I mean to go on with me running away, I was glad we were meeting in a public place, if I'd been at home you can't run away in your own home and if we'd been at his I wonder if he'd have let me go he might put me in a cupboard not really, anyway yes I got up and left and I kept thinking had he followed me.

SALTER   As you mean to go on as in not seeing him any more

B2   as in leaving the country.

SALTER   For what for a week or two a holiday, I don't

B2   leaving, going on yes I don't know, going away, I don't want to be here.

SALTER   But when you come back he'll still

B2   so maybe I won't

SALTER   but that's, not come back, no that's

B2   I don't know I don't know don't ask me I don't know. I'm going, I don't know. I don't want to be anywhere near him.

SALTER   You think he might try to hurt you?

B2   Why? why do you keep

SALTER   I don't know. Is it that?

B2   It's partly that, it's also it's horrible, I don't feel myself and there's the others

	too, I don't want to see them I don't want them
SALTER	I thought you did.
B2	I thought I did, I might, if I go away by myself I might feel all right, I might feel – you can understand that.
SALTER	Yes, yes I can.
B2	Because there's this person who's identical to me
SALTER	he's not
B2	who's not identical, who's like
SALTER	not even very
B2	not very like but very something terrible which is exactly the same genetic person
SALTER	not the same person
B2	and I don't like it.
SALTER	I know. I'm sorry.
B2	I know you're sorry I'm not
SALTER	I know
B2	I'm not trying to make you say sorry
SALTER	I know, I just am
B2	I know
SALTER	I just am sorry.
B2	He said some things.

SALTER   Yes.

B2   There's a lot of things I don't, could you tell me what happened to my mother?

SALTER   She's dead.

B2   Yes.

SALTER   I told you she was dead.

B2   Yes but she didn't die when I was born and she didn't die with the first child in a carcrash because the first child's not dead he's walking round the streets at night giving me nightmares. Unless she did die in a carcrash?

SALTER   No.

B2   No.

SALTER   Your mother, the thing a thing about your mother was that she wasn't very happy, she wasn't a very happy person at all, I don't mean there were sometimes days she wasn't happy or I did things that made her not happy I did of course, she was always not happy, often cheerful and

B2   she killed herself. How did she do that?

SALTER   She did it under a train under a tube train, she was one of those people when they say there has been a person under a train and the trains are delayed she was a person under a train.

B2	Were you with her?
SALTER	With her on the platform no, I was still *with* her more or less but not with her then no I was having a drink I think.
B2	And the boy?
SALTER	Do you know I don't remember where the boy was. I think he was at a friend's house, we had friends.
B2	And he was how old four?
SALTER	no no he was four later when I he was walking, about two just starting to talk
B2	he was four when you sent him
SALTER	that's right when his mother died he was two.
B2	So this was let me be clear this was before this was some years before I was born she died before
SALTER	yes
B2	so she was already always
SALTER	yes she was
B2	just so I'm clear. And then you and the boy you and your son
SALTER	we went on we just
B2	lived alone together
SALTER	yes

B2	you were bringing him up
SALTER	yes
B2	the best you could
SALTER	I
B2	until
SALTER	and my best wasn't very but I had my moments, don't think, I did cook meals now and then and read a story I'm sure I can remember a particularly boring and badly written little book about an elephant at sea. But I could have managed better.
B2	Yes he said something about it
SALTER	he said
B2	yes
SALTER	yes of course he did yes. I know I could have managed better because I did with you because I stopped, shut myself away, gave it all up came off it all while I waited for you and I think we may even have had that same book, maybe it's you I remember reading it to, do you remember it at all? it had an elephant in red trousers.
B2	No I don't think
SALTER	no it was terrible, we had far better books we had

B2	Maybe he shouldn't blame you, maybe it was a genetic, could you help drinking we don't know or drugs at the time philosophically as I understand it it wasn't viewed as not like now when our understanding's different and would a different person genetically different person not have been so been so vulnerable because there could always be some genetic addictive and then again someone with the same genetic exactly the same but at a different time a different cultural and of course all the personal all kinds of what happened in your own life your childhood or things all kind of because suppose you'd had a brother with identical an identical twin say but separated at birth so you had entirely different early you see what I'm saying would he have done the same things who can say he might have been a very loving father and in fact of course you have that in you to be that because you were to me so it's a combination of very complicated and that's who you were so probably I shouldn't blame you.
SALTER	I'd rather you blamed me. I blame myself.
B2	I'm not saying you weren't horrible.
SALTER	Couldn't I not have been?
B2	Apparently not.

SALTER	If I'd tried harder.
B2	But someone like you couldn't have tried harder. What does it mean? If you'd tried harder you'd have been different from what you were like and you weren't you were
SALTER	but then later I
B2	later yes
SALTER	I did try that's what I did I started again I
B2	that's what
SALTER	I was good I tried to be good I was good to you
B2	that's what you were like
SALTER	I was good
B2	but I can't you can't I can't give you credit for that if I don't give you blame for the other it's what you did it's what happened
SALTER	but it felt
B2	it felt
SALTER	it felt as if I tried I deliberately
B2	of course it felt
SALTER	well then
B2	it feels it always it feels doesn't it inside that's just how we feel what we are and

	we don't know all these complicated we can't know what we're it's too complicated to disentangle all the causes and we feel this is me I freely and of course it's true who you are does freely not forced by someone else but who you are who you are itself forces or you'd be someone else wouldn't you?
SALTER	I did some bad things. I deserve to suffer. I did some better things. I'd like recognition.
B2	That's how everyone feels, certainly.
SALTER	He still blames me.
B2	There's a difference then.
SALTER	You remind me of him.
B2	I remind myself of him. We both hate you.
SALTER	I thought you
B2	I don't blame you it's not your fault but what you've been like what you're like I can't help it.
SALTER	Yes of course.
B2	Except what he feels as hate and what I feel as hate are completely different because what you did to him and what you did to me are different things.
SALTER	I was nice to you.

B2   Yes you were.

SALTER   You don't have to go away. Not for long.

B2   It might make me feel better.

SALTER   I love you.

B2   That's something else you can't help.

SALTER   That's all right. That's all right.

B2   Also I'm afraid he'll kill me.

4

SALTER *and* BERNARD (B1).

SALTER So what kind of a place was it? was it

B1 the place

SALTER he was in a hotel was he or

B1 no

SALTER I thought he was in a hotel. So where was he?

B1 what?

SALTER I'm trying to get a picture.

B1 Does it matter?

SALTER It won't bring him back no obviously but I'd like I'd like you can't help feeling curious you want to get at it and you're blocked in all directions, your son dies you want his body, you want to know where his body last was when he was alive, you can't help

B1 He had a room.

SALTER In somebody's house, renting

B1 some small you know how the locals when you arrive, just a room not breakfast you'd go out for a coffee.

SALTER	So was it some pretty on a harbour front or
B1	no
SALTER	thinking of him on holiday
B1	in a street just a side
SALTER	but of course it wasn't a holiday he was hiding he thought he was hiding. Did you go inside the room?
B1	Just a small room, rather dark, one window and the shutters
SALTER	not very tidy I expect
B1	that's right, not tidy the bed not made, couple of books, bag on the floor with clothes half out of it
SALTER	did he scream?
B1	and you know what he's like, not tidy, am I tidy you don't know do you but you'd guess not wouldn't you but you'd be wrong there because I'm meticulous.
SALTER	What I want to know is how you actually, what you, how you got him to go off to some remote because that's what I'm imagining, you don't shoot the lodger without the landlady hearing, I don't know if you did shoot I don't know why I say shoot you could have had a knife you could have strangled, I can't think he would have gone off with you because he was frightened which is why

> but perhaps you talked you made him
> feel or did you follow him or lie in wait
> in some dark? and I don't know how
> you found him there did you follow him
> from his house when he left or follow
> him from here last time he?

B1   I didn't need to tell you it had happened

SALTER   but you did so naturally I want to

B1   and I'm wishing I hadn't

SALTER   no I'm glad

B1   and I'm not telling you

SALTER   because I won't tell anyone

B1   and there's nothing more to be said.

SALTER   What about the others? or is he the only
               one you hated because I loved him, I
               don't love the others, you and I have got
               common cause against the others don't
               forget, I'm still hoping we'll make our
               fortunes there. I'm going to talk to a
               solicitor, I've been too busy not busy but
               it's been like a storm going on I don't
               know what's gone on, it's not been very
               long ago it all started. You're not going
               to be a serial, wipe them all out so
               you're the only, back like it was at the
               start I'd understand that. If they do
               catch up with you, I'm sure they won't
               I'm sure you know what you're, if they
               do we'll tell them it was me it was my
               fault anyway you look at it. Don't you

agree, don't you feel that? Don't stop talking to me. It wasn't his fault, you should have killed me, it's my fault you. Perhaps you're going to kill me, is that why you've stopped talking? Shall I kill myself? I'd do that for you if you like, would you like that?

I'll tell you a thought, I could have killed you and I didn't. I may have done terrible things but I didn't kill you. I could have killed you and had another son, made one the same like I did or start again have a different one get married again and I didn't, I spared you though you were this disgusting thing by then anyone in their right mind would have squashed you but I remembered what you'd been like at the beginning and I spared you, I didn't want a different one, I wanted that again because you were perfect just like that and I loved you.

You know you asked me when you used to shout in the night. Sometimes I was there, I'd sit and listen to you or I'd not be in any condition to hear you I'd just be sitting. Sometimes I'd go out and leave you. I don't think you got out of bed, did you get out of bed, because you'd be frightened what I'd do to you so it was all right to go out. That was just a short period you used to shout, you grew out of that, you got so you'd rather not see me, you wanted to be left alone in the night, you wouldn't want me to come any more. You'd nearly stopped speaking do you remember that? not speaking not eating I tried to make you. I'd put you in the cupboard do you remember? or I'd look for you everywhere and I'd think you'd got away and I'd find you under the bed. You liked it there I'd put your dinner under for you. But it got worse do you remember? There was nobody but us. One day I cleaned you up and said take him into care. You didn't look too bad and they took you away. My darling. Do you remember that? Do you remember that day because I don't remember it you know. The whole thing is very vague to me. It's two years I remember almost nothing about but you must remember things and when you're that age two years is much longer, it wasn't very long to me, it was one long night out. Can you tell me anything you remember? the day you left? can you tell me things I did I might have forgotten?

B1   When I was following him there was a time I was getting on the same train and he looked round, I thought he was looking right at me but he didn't see me. I got on the train and went with him all the way.

SALTER   Yes? yes?

5

SALTER *and* MICHAEL BLACK, *his son, thirty-five.*

MICHAEL   Have you met the others?

SALTER   You're the first.

MICHAEL   Are you going to meet us all?

SALTER   I thought I'd start.

MICHAEL   I'm sure everyone will be pleased to meet you. I know I am.

SALTER   I'm sorry to stare.

MICHAEL   No, please, I can see it must be. Do I look like?

SALTER   Yes of course

MICHAEL   of course, I meant

SALTER   no no I didn't mean

MICHAEL   I suppose I meant how

SALTER   because of course you don't, you don't, not exactly

MICHAEL   no of course

SALTER   I wouldn't mistake

MICHAEL   no

SALTER   or I might at a casual

MICHAEL   of course

SALTER   but not if I really look

MICHAEL   no

SALTER   no

MICHAEL   because?

SALTER   because of the eyes. You don't look at me in the same way.

MICHAEL   I'm looking at someone I don't know of course.

SALTER   Maybe you could tell me a little

MICHAEL   about myself

SALTER   if you don't mind

MICHAEL   no of course, it's where to, you already know I'm a teacher, mathematics, you know I'm married, three children did I tell you that

SALTER   yes but you didn't

MICHAEL   boy and girl twelve and eight and now a baby well eighteen months so she's walking and beginning to talk, I don't have any photographs on me I didn't think, there's no need for photographs is there if you see someone all the time so

SALTER   are you happy?

MICHAEL   what now? or in general? Yes I think I am, I don't think about it, I am. The job gets me down sometimes. The world's a mess of course. But you can't help, a sunny morning, leaves turning, off to the park with the baby, you can't help feeling wonderful can you?

SALTER   Can't you?

MICHAEL Well that's how I seem to be.

SALTER   Tell me. Forgive me

MICHAEL no go on

SALTER   tell me something about yourself that's really specific to you, something really important

MICHAEL what sort of?

SALTER   anything

MICHAEL it's hard to

SALTER   yes.

MICHAEL Well here's something I find fascinating, there are these people who used to live in holes in the ground, with all tunnels and underground chambers and sometimes you'd have a chamber you'd get to it through a labyrinth of passages and the ceiling got lower and lower so you had to go on your hands and knees and then wriggle on your stomach and you'd get through to this chamber deep deep down that had a hole like a chimney like a well a hole all the way up to the sky so you could sit in this chamber this room this cave whatever and look up at a little circle of sky going past overhead. And when somebody died they'd hollow out more little rooms so they weren't buried underneath you they were buried in the walls beside you. And maybe sometimes they walled people up alive in there, it's possible because of how the remains were contorted but either way of course they're dead by now and very soon after they went in of course. And

SALTER   I don't think this is what I'm looking for

MICHAEL   oh, how, sorry

SALTER   because what you're telling me is about something else and I was hoping for something about you

MICHAEL   I don't quite

SALTER   I'm sorry I don't know I was hoping

MICHAEL   you want what my beliefs, politics how I feel about war for instance is that? I dislike war, I'm not at all happy when people say we're doing a lot of good with our bombing, I'm never very comfortable with that. War's one of those things, don't you think, where everyone always thinks they're in the right have you noticed that? Nobody ever says we're the bad guys, we're going to beat shit out of the good guys. What do you think?

SALTER   I was hoping I don't know something more personal something from deep inside your life. If that's not intrusive.

MICHAEL   Maybe what maybe my wife's ears?

SALTER   Yes?

MICHAEL   Because last night we were watching the news and I thought what beautiful and slightly odd ears she's got, they're small but with big lobes, big relative to the small ear, and they're slightly pointy on top, like a disney elf or little animal ears and they're always there but you know how you suddenly notice and noticing that, I mean the way I love her, felt very felt what you said something deep inside. Or the children obviously, I could talk about, is this the sort of thing?

SALTER   it's not quite

MICHAEL   no

SALTER   because you're just describing other people or

MICHAEL   yes

SALTER   not yourself

MICHAEL   but it's people I love so

SALTER   it's not what I'm looking for. Because anyone could feel

MICHAEL   oh of course I'm not claiming

SALTER   I was somehow hoping

MICHAEL   yes

SALTER   further in

MICHAEL   yes

SALTER   just about yourself

MICHAEL   myself

SALTER   yes

MICHAEL   like maybe I'm lying in bed and it's comfortable and then it gets slightly not so comfortable and I move my legs or even turn over and then it's

SALTER   no

MICHAEL   no

SALTER   no that's

MICHAEL   yes that's something everyone

SALTER   yes

MICHAEL   well I don't know. I like blue socks. Banana icecream. Does that help you?

SALTER   Dogs?

MICHAEL   do I like

SALTER   dogs

MICHAEL   I'm ok with dogs. My daughter wants a puppy but I don't know. Is dogs the kind of thing?

SALTER   So tell me what did you feel when you found out?

MICHAEL Fascinated.

SALTER   Not angry?

MICHAEL No.

SALTER   Not frightened.

MICHAEL No, what of?

SALTER   Your life, losing your life.

MICHAEL I've still got my life.

SALTER   But there are things there are things that are what you are, I think you're avoiding

MICHAEL yes perhaps

SALTER   because then you might be frightened

MICHAEL I don't think

SALTER   or angry

MICHAEL not really

SALTER   because what does it do what does it to you to everything if there are all these walking around, what it does to me what am I and it's not even me it happened to, so how you can just, you must think something about it.

MICHAEL I think it's funny, I think it's delightful

SALTER   delightful?

MICHAEL   all these very similar people doing things like each other or a bit different or whatever we're doing, what a thrill for the mad old professor if he'd lived to see it, I do see the joy of it. I know you're not at all happy.

SALTER   I didn't feel I'd lost him when I sent him away because I had the second chance. And when the second one my son the second son was murdered it wasn't so bad as you'd think because it seemed fair. I was back with the first one.

MICHAEL   But now

SALTER   now he's killed himself

MICHAEL   now you feel

SALTER   now I've lost him, I've lost

MICHAEL   yes

SALTER   now I can't put it right any more. Because the second time round you see I slept very lightly with the door open.

MICHAEL   Is that the worst you did, not go in the night?

SALTER   No of course not.

MICHAEL   Like what?

SALTER   Things that are what I did that are not trivial like banana icecream nor unifuckingversal like turning over in bed.

MICHAEL   We've got ninety-nine per cent the same genes as any other person. We've got ninety per cent the same as a chimpanzee. We've got thirty percent the same as a lettuce. Does that cheer you up at all? I love about the lettuce. It makes me feel I belong.

SALTER   I miss him so much. I miss them both.

MICHAEL   There's nineteen more of us.

SALTER   That's not the same.

MICHAEL   No of course not. I was making a joke.

SALTER   And you're happy you say are you? you like your life?

MICHAEL   I do yes, sorry.